The Field in Winter

David Clensy

The Field in Winter

David Clarke

Nine
Arches
Press

The Field in Winter
David Clarke

ISBN: 978-1-913437-76-3
eISBN: 978-1-913437-77-0

First published September 2023 by:

Nine Arches Press
Unit 14, Sir Frank Whittle Business Centre,
Great Central Way, Rugby.
CV21 3XH
United Kingdom

www.ninearchespress.com

Printed on recycled paper in the United Kingdom
by Imprint Digital.

Nine Arches Press is supported using public funding
by Arts Council England.

Supported using public funding by
**ARTS COUNCIL
ENGLAND**

In memory of my father,
John Frederick Clarke
(1944-2021)

Contents

Reciting a Poem by Czesław Miłosz at Krasnogruda

for Krzysztof Czyżewski

The first thing I want to tell you about
is the trunk of this linden tree –
the surprise of its having taken up
a whole day's heat from the earth
through the wick of its cracked skin.

Then, at my feet, there are ants
in a web of leaves, twigs and dust,
busy in their unknowable world.
The villagers line up to speak
the poet's words, which I do not

understand fully in any language.
I've chosen one of his last, taking it
as confession of doubt that drove him.
The villagers listen politely as I stumble
over the poem's uneven threshold –

If I could at last tell you what is in me.
These words turn for a moment in my mind
before the tongue can catch them, briefly,
on their flight through birch and thicket,
to ignite the lake's dark eye.

After the Plum Harvest

August has turned blue to black.
Bulbs of syrupy liquor droop,
pendulous on brittle staves.
Welts in flesh that will not scar –

they open, glisten to the wasps
who tumble, twitchy-limbed
to lap at ooze. Now amber tears
run dry and make a tacky gum.

The sun is low.
It silhouettes drab sacks of skin
that wither in the canopy.
Is summer still inside?

They drop through green
and mulch the earth with boozy rot.

"Sweetie"

The children carry a cage beneath the trees,
coo and call to the runaway,
rattle a dish of his favourite seed.

They've learned the charm of words
we use to keep our dear ones close
when we've been careless with their hearts.

Darling, lover, only we croon,
our voices pale with fear they'll fly
like this small bird that lights its flame

in highest branches, unimagined sky,
hearing distant voices of those he knew,
his own sweet name lost in the dusk.

First Time Swimming in the Lake at Krasnogruda

A night of storm. Then morning gently struck
the prayer bowl of the sun. Its chime resolved
to silence. Hot, rough boards beneath my feet
as light rocked on the black expanse.

Vision shattered into countless planes,
each one a partial mirror of the world.
Halfway down the ladder, my shocked spine
became conductor of the water's cold,

as if the static of thunder clung to my bones.
My mind was a defective bulb,
my self unmade and remade
in the space of a breath. I pushed away

from rusted metal, murk and weed,
heard a heart that hammered for release.

A Stork at Krasnogruda

This bird is all beak,
a blade aligned to the eye.
Pacing fields with a surgeon's tact,
it lances movement in stubble.

Flight is an unfurling –
the body's grubby parasol
flung into the heavens.
A pale death drags its shadow

over land and water,
alights in a boneyard nest
to toss the chicks their morsels.
At sundown it settles among them,

wrapped in its bleached frockcoat.
The night will sheathe its mind.

The Path from Krasnogruda to Ogrodniki

Wine and echo and argument
roll from a doorway's mouth of gold.
Our torch beams lurch through trees
and sweep the ground. Before us, tiny frogs

scatter and bounce like silver change.
Now our words are tangled
in summer's mesh of lichen and leaf.
The forest moves with industries

that silence us, reduce our progress
to scuff of boots on gravel
as we carry the moon on our backs.
For all that we have said, the world

is never close. Still, we sense it now
and dare not shy it with a whisper.

A Spider in My Kitchen

In the cupboard with the spices,
those half-used packs of rice and beans,
a spider rules the dark, her hind parts
dabbed in gauze – the cache of eggs.

I do not want her in my house,
but she is calligraphed on air,
not bristling thick for scooping
in a jar. What is this wish

for riddance without harm?
That feeling finally needs a name.
The spider casts a creamy net
to swaddle up her young. They float,

transparent lice, like all the dormant
mischief that will wreck the world.

Flies

Such intricate corpses –
they rustled on the sill in drifts,
bludgeoned by their own wrong-headed
butting at the windows.

All summer they'd filled this room,
summoned from nothing like nasty thoughts.
I heard them from behind the door
and thought of meat and jewels.

Then I found the mouse,
skin dried taut across its ribs.
Escaping the cat, it must have crawled
inside the fireplace to die

then birthed these other furious lives –
it grimaced from the effort.

Before Storm Ellen Arrives

This premonition has swollen in days of heat.
Now neighbours lean from windows
to see the tempest fanfare its own birth.
All the birds are quitting the sky.

A great yew bucks and thrashes like a bear
in chains. Cudgelled by blasts of grey air,
it flashes grim and powerless paws.
Shirt-spectres twist on washing lines.

Streets are skittered with leaves and plastic bags.
The skyline sparks to negative and groans,
makes every house quake. The bones
of people are kindling now,

dry as twigs that brute boys snap
in rushes of senseless, sudden strength.

Before Storm Ellen Leaves

The road is wild as the lid of a boiling pot.
Tarmac writhes like a channel for black eels.
Land and sky are either water
or steam. Houses curl and cower.

Thunder breaks open another magnum of froth.
Every leaf and lamp and downpipe
drips syncopated beats. Beasts
of field and hedgerow wait for the end,

stretch their noses into warmer hours.
Time runs into gutters, churns itself
green. Hills swell, shift their sodden
coats about old shoulders, sigh.

Merciful storm. Pull us softly apart
and sluice us. We are open to earth.

Rabbit

He swung the brace on bright green twine,
blind heads knocking against his shin.
He showed us nick-by-cut to free
the pelt, peeled back to marbled blue.

Slit chin to tail, I opened a purse
that spilled its trove in mucous and gall.
The gut held up its necklace of scats,
the bladder swung a sack of gold.

Then on the bones meat seared in smoke,
spat fat on embers, shrivelled, charred.
I carried the stench for days on my hands,
a burr that chafed at the back of my throat.

Starlings at Royal Well

I remember striking metal fences,
tensile wires to make the sci-fi sounds
of lasers deep in space. Those chill
vibrations shivered in my chest

and tuned the mind to frequencies like these –
a swirl of starlings rolling in to roost
inside this spread of sycamores,
a cumulus of black and green

that ripples with their quarrel and complaint.
Now the twilight is made of birds.
They hoard the shadow in these crowns
and call down night with urgency.

I fill my lungs with jangling air,
carry it home to shake my sleepless hours.

Fen Lane

I walk to where the tarmac runs out
to runnels of slurry and clay,
beyond the void of playing fields,
those last few desolate houses.

Here cider drinkers make their dens
in hollows of coat-ripping thicket.
A pink sock flaps in razor wire
around a substation's hum.

Water climbs the banks of the cut,
sodden as fly-tipped mattresses,
and cows in the middle-distance turn
their woeful heads to size me up.

If I wander much further now,
I might never be heard from again.

Fog in Byron Road

This morning there is no world
beyond the end of our street.
Each house is a model of itself,
too precise to be believed.

Time suspended might sound like this –
a door slammed is echoless gunfire,
children call out from their padded cells.
Now a flock of doves careens –

a whiteness made from whiteness,
pulsing in and out of view.
Its wheezing machine reels close,
contracts, expands –

a conjuror who shows us
the nothing in his hand.

Clais Fhearnaig

The moment after the world was shaken
this rubble bounced like dice across
a baize of spongey heather, dropped
into the lochan's rusty well,

where chunks of granite are sinking still –
unheard the final clunk of contact
that would measure depth in time.
But in the shallows each knuckle's haired

in umber weed. The current laps
soft waves of cold against my shins.
Here a man could petrify,
his fires chilled to such hard stuff

hands of water neither shape
nor force his stony mind to speak.

November

I love you for plaguing
the council contractor
who ripped out
an awkward tree
yards from our door –
until they planted
this hornbeam that grows,
narrow as a boy,
new in our sight.
They chose it,
I imagine,
for its modest claim
on earth and sky.
But – oh! –
autumn makes it
ecstatic,
brandishing leaves
of old gold,
like flames in the icon
of a martyrdom.
This year's season
is too warm.
The tree turns late.
The world now seems
to tilt and shake
beneath us.

We have few days
before the cold
will cast this beauty
at our worthless feet –
so little time to spend
our awe on treasure.

Fog at Auborn

The road has unlearned
the shape I knew,
spins out curves to snare me.
Bottomless ditches gape.

I slow to a funeral pace.
My muffled engine
drums impatient fingers.
I push through solid light.

In hedgerow someone flips
a disc of gold – hare eye,
panicked, flares across my path.
Muscle slaloms handlamps.

Leaning forward,
I see my terror run.

Picking Sloes

Into blackthorn's delicate snare
we dip our hands and pluck the fruits
that pucker as autumn cools. Inside
this complication of pricking tines,
bitterness glows, dense and heady
as the rites of a moribund cult.

These worry beads slip from their threads,
weightless into plastic bags,
becoming heavy there as if
we carried game-sacks home to skin.
When we climb the lane at dusk
they thud against our shins.

In the kitchen, spirit sleeps,
a green sun captured in its flasks.
Our fingers stained, we heap the hoard
that we have saved from these last days.
Mounds of sugar wait to polish
shine into the purple of sloes.

The Field in Winter

Where once was field, the flood
has broken bounds. Ditch and road
are one grey film. Wind ruts
in divots sheep have made

and hedges shred black plastic,
expose the nests of season's end.
The earth is deep, unwalkable –
a mire to suck you down

and tan you in the land's brown juice.
A thousand years of empty sleep
will leave you wizened, pungent,
the head gone springy as a nut.

By then the field's forgotten
all your kind. A final blessing.

A Spider's Web on Exmoor

An opening of heather frames
a rhizome stitched from dew,
fine as cattle-breath in frost.
Pearls of blossom blush amber to pink.

Water rushes through this land
and now we've stopped, we feel it give
like horsehair stuffed in an antique bed,
all oaken scent of whisky corks.

The wind is picking at our clothes
and at the wool in wire fences.
This web distorts, still waits
for tiny deaths to prick its nerves.

In certain weather, we see the space
between all things.

Old Dalby

White blades divide the air
on their barren promontory.
They glance this planet's force,

as I might press my hand
against a river's torrent.
An A-road roars beneath,

a hissing flow of metal –
the movement we have invented
to not be still with our selves.

Each turbine's bevelled shaft
is rooted in ploughed earth.
They have the drone of prayer-wheels

which we may hope to turn
in absence of final answer.

Liniment

When I was still growing, my shins would ache.
        Bone stretched to fit a new life.

Then my father would come to my sleepless room
        with an oldfangled bottle of embrocation

to palm away that almost pleasant pain,
        anoint me with a locker-room stink,

and leave me gently burning inside my skin.
        Later, we rarely touched (men don't, I'm told) –

until his final hour. Then I placed
        my hand on his forearm, between the sleeve

of his hospital gown and the blue blanket.
        And if we have love it is this – to know the struggle

of another body, with our hands
        to soothe each transformation.

The Word Box

I carried a tobacco tin home from school
and tipped its slips of paper onto the table –
a teacher's biro spelled what I had to learn,
that broken magic I'd use to make a world.

My father kept bolts and tacks in tins,
fixings to hold whatever we needed in place.
He loved a line that was plumb and clean,
to fit parts surely into his neat designs.

I opened the word box day on day,
but never had his knack of hand and eye.
Timber split, stone would not lie straight,
but what I shaped with words was odder still.

And now my father cannot mend when I fail.
His tools are idle in the dark. I make
no sense, but take the measure of grief
and find my work is always out of true.

Anniversary

I take my breaths of these twelve months
and fill a sky where nobody lives,
its half-moon catching invisible sun.
Black poplars are smeared with mistletoe,
shadows on an X-rayed lung.

Down here, the mulch of earth and grass
is sharp and true as rising dough.
Twilight's a blue that's sweet to inhale,
a copper penny tang on the gums.
Even my sad body is praise.

Today, I remember how you refused
the struggle for air, when all they offered
was bottled and dripped to sterile machines.
I draw a world into me now,
taste the promise of the turning year.

February

I stepped across the threshold
        into a world of cold,
as carefully as if I entered
        a sleeping infant's room.

Instead of dawn, I saw the sky
        shift from Marian
to Egyptian blue.
        In fields and woods, the snow

had gathered acres of light.
        I dreamed I walked into that daze
and laid my body down.
        I had an empty mind of ice,

a silent tongue of ice.
        And in that fever
I let myself be sung,
        then, like a song, dissolve.

The Severn by Sedbury

Rearing over a tump of grass –
a craft. It cups its years of sand,
a shapely palm of fibreglass
blown watery blue by briny wind.

Its other freight is one frayed net,
the whole of the sky. Oarless,
it still seems to heave a course
across the current's sly demands.

It does not rest upon that dune,
remembers still the lurch of tides,
human shapes it bore
into a lantern-swinging gloom.

Poor boat. I see no hands to haul
your shining cargo clear.

After Impact

An etching splayed on cold glass,
intricate as ice on shallow water.
It shimmers like feathered breath or smoke
hung in the window's white frame.

What was it that collided with our house?
That sparrowhawk, shaking itself on the lawn?
More likely, a missing spirit
who circles us in loops of love.

We trace the idea of it in the pane,
imagine ether becoming body,
ringing the cracked bell of this world.
It leaves us baffled, witnesses of grace.

The Field in Spring

Say this piece of land's an eye
a sleeping king has closed
upon his realm. Say it flickers
now in March, as vision moves

beneath the membrane, a synapse
twitching at the touch of light.
Say it opens wide and is a mirror,
trapping silver in its troubled pool.

Clouds are racing through it,
a dance the earth itself becomes.
The shoulders roll, the belly heaves –
a ponderous gavotte.

The weary monarch stumbles to reign,
reclaims his ruined crown.

Starlings in the Garden

Moulded sleek for water more than air,
I think, they dive the depth of morning –
a quill of arrows loosed into a battle.
Wideboys in from nowhere, they strut

in tonic suits, give clannish nods and winks.
Tender then they offer scraps
to feed their fluffed-up, idiot young.
Their own quick greed's a gulping down of life.

Each head-jerk winds the body tighter,
tensed for flight. A window opens
and they explode into sky,
vanish like a thought I could not hold.

When I step into the sun, they eye me
from a darkness under leaves.

Cherry Blossom

Not stars – but then no poem can begin
with what is not. Step forward to observe
the five foils of each flower, toothpaste white
and shuddering – sensation that withholds

all tender language. Blossom blossoms,
and yet the data of each petal slides
beneath our names, leaving only form
and movement – a breeze that frets the surface

of an opaque pool. I cannot navigate
by such refusal. It sloughs off all coordinates.
It leaves me floating as a focused eye
and makes that eye a singular bloom

or pulse of wild and ancient light –
and so perhaps a star then, after all.

Coult Avenue

Here I am. In the front room of my grandparents' house. An afternoon of nearly summer warms through windows the dog has tongue- and nose-smeared. Sun textures the flaking sofa, opens the empty grate. A butt unwinds its final ribbon of smoke from the ashtray by a cold cup. And in that cup, dark leaves fleck milky dregs. They shake a little as I step from shadow – the queasy film of their surface like a smaller window into the room. Being for the first time myself, I arrive with not a question in my mind, no memory of how I came to stand here in this sudden body. I listen for my young aunts, who at any moment may thunder down the stairs into the hall, slam a door, or turn up their transistors. That choking smell of hairspray and damp coal. A car pulls up outside. The whole world is waiting for my next move.

Before the Plum Harvest

I test their flesh with my fingers.
A young wine's purple gleams
beneath the bloom I rub away.
If the stem will give them gently,

if they roll into my grasp,
there may be sun enough within.
But when I force, they green against
my teeth. A smack of wood-sap

dries my mouth and leaves a naked
stone to spit among tall grass.
Some I pluck from ripening's cusp –
hardness gives way to fresh surprise,

a stream that runs from tart
to clear. The drink I need.

Sunken Lane

Descending from the afternoon
into a shaft of root and earth,
I stumble over stones rubbed slick
by tides of cartwheel, boot and hoof.

The canopy tightens over me,
winnows blue through shifting leaves.
The banks rear up and smother thought.
Sweat is chilling in my clothes.

I hear blood pumping through my head.
Roots coil to tripwires in the loam.
I'm pulled towards a point of light,
a gate that opens onto glare.

Beyond it surely the world is changed.
I've been away for many years.

The Bees

Walk with me under the limes.
There's something I want you to know –
each tree is a quaking dome

when the frenzied bees are at work,
snug bodies suckling blossom.
They toil in shadow and sing

with their selves, delight
of this ideal arrangement,
limbs dusted with future perfections.

How we long for labour like this –
to lose our days in the making of life,
to honey the air with our joy.

The Fall

Slant across this mongrel brook,
an ash is anchored to one bank
by half its roots. The rest grasp air,
as if they could be planted there.

In those moments since ground gave way,
since age or storm propelled this life
towards its end, a cushion of green
has spread across the trunk.

Where sunlight makes a tenderness,
some common moss, fronds of bluebell
gleam in a skein of loam and rot.
New ivy places tiny hearts.

And as I duck to follow the track,
the tree rests briefly upon my back.
I press my palm against warm bark,
as if I'd somehow ease this fall.

Crow

The hill stands open like a house in summer.
And there is my soul,
        riding the ragged winds.

He has put away his shriek, his claws,
becomes a chord
        played in the music of air.

He knows that he is fashioned from darkness,
yet now he is caught
        in a greater movement

that sweeps him briefly beyond desire.
The current ebbs.
        He plummets to seek the earth,

the business of hunger sharp in his eye.
I hold my breath,
        spread my wings wide.

Advice for Those Who Are Not Yet Fifty Years Old

First, do not ask me for advice –
how I came to this place,
stumbling from the maze of years
onto this bright field

with its miraculous horizon,
that is all a mystery to me.
There were no triumphs
but somehow my mistakes were forgiven

by a kindly world.
All I can tell you then
is that I woke one morning
to find someone beside me

to whom I could say *Yes*
with all of my being.
My one wise decision
was to hold onto that.

Accident

This is not how he imagined rebirth –
his body flailing through cold space,
tarmac's sickening impact.

But when he woke, full grown
and goofy as a foal, he shone
in the haze of arrival.

And when he could walk,
he went every day to the park
for the joy of sitting under trees.

Now he says his mind is a river.
The spine of his history is broken
and the glassy current spins its pages

beyond his reach. With them float
the hurts his shyness hid,
each reason not to open himself

to love. Just this fragment
remains – light, water,
his hand in his father's hand.

Mahonia Blossom

Pine sap, cat's piss, sherbet.
A dusty candelabra.
Heliodor in a spiky brooch.
Wax in the angel's ear.

Butter on Lucifer's toast.
Bee music.
The curse's active ingredient.
A mild chastisement.

A strong sedative,
its queasy side-effects.
The too much of everything.
A tin of mustard.

A box of matches.
The fires I've started.

Urban Fox

Mid-morning, she saunters up garden paths,
noses into shrubs for grease-smeared
bags and foils. Her coat has coarsened.
She lopes like a comfortable hound

who'll never need that bigger brain
of forebears who haunted glittering fields,
who pounced on quivering prey,
moved like a rumour in and out of the trees.

But sometimes she also stops beneath
a streetlight, turns her head to hear
the call of a greater life.

Toad Lesson

What did you mean to tell me, toad,
when you made yourself from dust
and leaves beneath my spade?
You flexed inside your mottled bag of skin,
dragged yourself towards the hedge.

I thought I'd spooked an ancestor –
as if their softness found me guilty,
the rough shaft in my trembling hand.
Now, I suppose you only basked,
offering the sun your back,
your dull nub of a head to warm.

I too would like to learn a life
that presses its belly to the ground,
finds itself sufficient. Forgive me.
Every day I wield sharp tools.
To live, I break and turn the earth.

Wake

The body always arrives first
announced by its own hot heft,
which gathers bed, chair, door,
and the window where motes of skin
swirl like plankton.

Only then, what we call mind
judders back to present fullness,
begins to name vibrations –
the dog's frantic bark, a neighbour
who hammers reality into place.

The Path from Ogrodniki to Krasnogruda

This dirt track parts humid air,
fuses a circuit of eye and loin.
Night has eaten from my flesh –
its bites are little flares

igniting with every step.
Sunlight sparks on chips of mica
in the sand. When I turn,
black branches shift,

mist releases light in hollows.
After-rain has spiced my tongue.
The body's delta
floods with tremor –

a wave of self at last set free.
Against the mind's hard no, a surge of *now*.

Second Time Swimming in the Lake at Krasnogruda

I open the book of the lake to read my body,
find it cool and green, a thought unrolled
in muscle at every stroke. Provisional,
its propositions constantly revised

by breeze that kneads the water into ripples,
or birds who clatter out of reeds like fear
that blunders through a dream. Back there on land,
who knows me? My dry arrangement speaks

his text and stalks the scene. The shape of me
extends in new dimensions here. My lungs,
like fluttered wings, press air from my chest.
The afternoon has drawn this circle wide –

its bright horizon pitches as I fold
the future's weight and find my way is free.

Another Stork at Krasnogruda

We build a tower for you, stork,
to set our rickety luck on –
a garland of broken things.
By season's end your young

will shit it grey and white as cloud.
We bid you stay a century
to sentinel our sleep
then skim your noontide silhouette

over this miserly earth,
so it may give us cream and chives
to savour our soup.
Let our age be slow and full.

Let the yard grow fat with babies.
Let history look the other way.

The day the soldiers come

they'll give you twenty minutes to pack.
Think now what you'll need

without this place you call home.
And remember the woman too stunned
by those uniformed men,

who smoked and laughed in her kitchen,
to use that precious time.
She sat by the cold grate

while her boy packed one suitcase.
She opened it weeks later
in a cold and hopeless land

to find no cook pots, scarves or pickles,
but a clockwork train, coloured pencils,
an atlas of constellations.

Marginal

All history has a hinterland –
those villages where news of succession
arrives by donkey, two years after
the old king was sealed in his tomb;

those valleys where people leave
their houses to watch a plane pass low,
know war from their one recruit,
who hobbles, blighted, back to his plough.

Which brings me to my grandparents,
who heard a bomb that overshot
a target of some real importance
and used their bodies to shelter

the cradle that held my father.
Inhaling his milky skin,
they heard their own hearts beating
in the silence before the blast.

In Wartime

Who dares to speak today of crocuses?
Their purple banners ripple in morning cold.

Closed, they augur coming heat, how flowers
ease apart to show yolk-yellow stigma

in their deepest fold. Inside the houses,
news breaks bones, as every day it must.

Loving this world, we know, is no way out.
But still, we guard the gift of our attention,

lest it be wracked upon the mind of power.
We seek a gentle reflex towards the day.

Glen Quoich

The new path spills across the valley's flank
as if a bag of boiled sweets has burst.
Each lump of granite has a sugar gleam,
veins of glister running deep inside.

My boots are coated in sickly dust.
I pick my way down sliding swathes of rock
and past the quarry where the stones were cut –
a tongue of boulders lolls across the glen.

I know whatever ways we make can't last.
Cobbles skitter as if to race me home.
(A glacier cracking as it calves. The clack
of giant rosaries.) And still I walk

in hope the weight of every step
could yet bed down the coming years.

The Severn by Waldings Pill

That stump is buried half inside
a bank that breaches the water's pull,
like an ancient flint harpoon
scarred into a whale's thick hide.

Weather-felled and hollowed
in the swell of flood, flayed
by river's slow design, it juts –
a last grey tooth inside a sinner's head.

This is the centre of the world.
It holds horizon's focus,
soft banks of undulating mud,
white birds that dip and reel. And I

am in the water, in the wood
and air, but find no shelter there.

Incident on Coldstream Terrace

A body keeps the shape of a body
even under a white tarpaulin,
even when it's dragged from the Taff,
a river grey as stone-cold tea
and gross with all the rain in Wales.

Laid on a concrete ramp, the body
slowly gets used to new thingness,
its power to draw the eye and open
the story we all know – that lovely
silence in water, the pull of an ocean

called *after life*. It spools its empty
frames through the mind's projector.
Policemen scribble into their pads,
quiz two pale and shivering men,
damp to their shins and tangled now

forever in a stranger's wake.
They will not go to work today,
but walk home slowly to houses
empty of everything they love.
From their windows they will watch

the sun scorch clouds to sugar pink,
plum purple, gold. Their hearts
will jump when post slaps onto the mat
and quicken again at evening
to hear a key turn in the door.

In the Street of Late Evening

I almost forgot to mention the bark of a cherry
in the halogen light of that new streetlamp.
How this made the tree more like a fractured
landscape – the wound of its slow eruption,
the agony of shedding skin inadequate
to its final form. This is trivial,
I realise – the tree a passing shape,
this world a doomed form of knowing.

By which I mean, my world. Still, there seems
no option but to grieve this coming loss,
how we will fail to save our only vision.
Without us, no beauty will arrest and change
a human eye. This mattered at that moment
very much, and somehow not at all.

While the tree-self shimmered or exhaled
in that denatured glow, the dog scouted
grass nearby, beholden to his houndscape
of odours, its bursts of anticipation.

Song

I thought the dawn said run,
        but it said rise.

I thought the sky said storm,
        but it said sail.

I thought the road said hard,
        but it said heart.

I thought the rock said break,
        but it said breathe.

I thought the raven said die,
        but he said thrive.

I thought the fire said burn,
        but it said bloom.

I thought the rain said cold,
        but it said clear.

I thought the night said fear,
        but it said flow.

I thought my mind
        was all the language I'd need,
                but I was mishearing the world.
So, I walked into the forest and

knew when the tree said timber,
       it meant limb.

And knew when the doe said danger,
       she meant dreamer.

And knew when the rowan said blood,
       it meant blessed.

And knew when the mud said filth,
       it meant faith.

I'd thought the earth was a sorrow.
       Also, it is a psalm.

The End of Summer

Love, you know I sometimes find my self
a labour too hard. And yet, this morning the radar
of my heart longed for the contours of the world.
I walked outside and saw two crows, who basked
on pantiles, blacker somehow for the sun.

The dog ducked through a hedge to run that path
through corn, bleached gold to white like his small body,
like droughted clay his paws percussed.

In teeming lanes, we gathered seeds on fabric
and fur, then doubled back to the shadowed pond,
shook off this new adornment as we strode.
We must have drawn a line across the land.
Not visible yet, but shining soon.

Acknowledgements and Thanks

Some of these poems (or earlier versions of them) appeared in *Fenland Reed*, *Buzzwords*, *Raceme*, *Dear Earth* (Frosted Fire Press), *Atrium*, *Ink, Sweat & Tears*, *Spelt* and *Under the Radar*. Many thanks to the editors and publishers for giving a home to my work.

In the summer of 2019, I was lucky enough to be the guest of the Borderland Foundation in Sejny and Krasnogruda, Poland. I am grateful in particular to Krzysztof Czyżewski, Małgorzata Sporek-Czyżewska, Weronika Czyżewska-Poncyljusz and Agata Szkopińska for their support during my stay.

The poem quoted in 'Reciting a Poem by Czesław Miłosz at Krasnogruda' is Miłosz's 'This' from *New and Collected Poems 1931–2001* (Penguin, 2001), pp. 663–664.

'The day the soldiers come' was inspired by Dalia Cidzikaitė, Dalia Stakė Anysas and Laima Petrauskas Vanderstoep, *We Thought We'd Be Back Soon: 18 Stories of Refugees 1940–1944* (Aukso žuvys, 2017).

My thanks go to the following poets who commented on earlier drafts of some of this work: Alison Brackenbury, Jonathan Davidson, Jennie Farley, Adam Horovitz, Lesley Ingram, Nina Lewis, Michael Loveday, Rowan Middleton and Philip Rush; and to Jane Commane for her brilliant editing and her encouragement of my work.

Finally, for his constant love and support, I am deeply grateful to Malcolm Allison.